Salads from around the world

SALADS

So much variety exists among salads that it is somewhat difficult to give a comprehensive definition of this class of foods. In general, however, They are food mixtures either arranged on a plate or tossed and served with a moist dressing. A dish of green herbs or vegetables, sometimes cooked, and usually chopped or sliced, sometimes mixed with fruit or with cooked and chopped cold meat, fish, etc. They are usually served with a dressing. It can be either hot or cold. The selection of salad ingredients depends upon seasons. Salads are unique. They can either accompany a main course, act as an appetizer, served as an extra party dish, or just plain served alone. A high-protein salad, such as lobster salad, replaces the meat course, whereas, a light salad of vegetables or fruits may be used as an additional course. For the most part, salads take their name from their chief ingredient, as, for instance, chicken salad, tomato salad, pineapple salad, etc. Just what place salads have in the meal depends on the salad itself.

SALADS IN THE DIET

Salads are often considered to be a dish of little importance; that is, something that is added to a meal. While this is the case with meals composed of a sufficient variety of foods, salads have a definite place in majority of households. Often there is a tendency to limit green vegetables or fresh fruits in the diet, but if the members of a family are to be fed an ideal diet it is extremely important that some of them are included in each day's meals. The most effective and appetizing way to include them in a meal is the serving of salads. One who gives much attention to the artistic side of the serving of food will often use a salad to carry out a color scheme in the meal. This is, of course, the least valuable use that salads have, but it is a point that should not be overlooked. The chief purpose of salads in a meal is to provide something that the rest of the foods served in the meal lack.

Although salads, through their variety, offer an opportunity to vary meals, it requires a little attention in selecting them if a properly balanced meal is to be served. Salads that are high in food value or contain ingredients similar to those found in the other dishes served in the meal, should be avoided with dinners or with other heavy meals. For instance, a fish or a meat salad should not be served with a dinner, for it would supply a quantity of protein to a meal that is already sufficiently high in this food substance because of the fact that meat also is included. Such a salad, however, has a place in a very light luncheon or supper, for it helps to balance such a meal. The best salad to be served with a dinner that contains a number of heavy dishes is a vegetable salad, if enough vegetables are not already included, or a fruit salad, if the dessert does not consist of fruit. In case a fruit salad is selected, it is often made to serve for both the salad and the dessert course.

If the meal is a light one and the salad is to be served as the principal dish, it should be sufficiently heavy and contain enough food value to serve the purpose for which it is intended. On the other hand when the meal is a heavy one it is always better to chose a lighter salad. For instance, with meat or fish as the main course of the meal, a fish, egg, or cheese salad would obviously be the wrong thing to serve. Instead, a light salad of vegetables or fruits should be selected for such a meal. It should be remembered that if the other dishes of a meal contain sufficient food value to make the meal properly nourishing, a salad containing a rich dressing will provide more than a sufficient supply of calories and consequently should be avoided. Another point that should not be neglected in selecting a salad is that it should be in contrast to the rest of the meal as far as flavor is concerned. While several foods acid in flavor do not necessarily unbalance a meal so far as food substances and food value are concerned, they provide too much of the same flavor to be agreeable to most persons. For instance, if the meal contains an acid soup, such as tomato, and a vegetable with a sour dressing, such as beets, then a salad that is also acid will be likely to add more of a sour flavor than the majority of persons desire.

COMPOSITION OF SALADS

One of the advantages of salads is that the ingredients from which they can be made are large in number. In fact, almost any cooked or raw fruit or vegetable, or any meat, fowl, or fish, whether cooked expressly for this purpose or left over from a previous meal, may be utilized in the making of salads. The composition, as well as the total food value, of salads depends entirely on the ingredients of which they are composed. An understanding of the composition of the ingredients used in salads will enable us to judge fairly accurately whether the salad is low, medium, or high in food value, and whether it is high in protein, fat, or carbohydrate. This matter is important, and should receive consideration from all who prepare this class of food.

Fruits, both canned and raw, are largely used in the making of salads. As with vegetables, almost any combination of them makes a delicious salad when served with the proper dressing. salads that are high in protein have for their basis, or contain, such ingredients as me a t , fish, fowl, cheese, eggs, nuts, or dried beans. As far as meats are concerned, they are not used so extensively in salads as are fruits and vegetables. The amount of protein such a salad contains naturally varies with the quantity of high-protein food that is used. The fat in salads is more often included as a part of the dressing than in any other way, but the quantity introduced may be very large. A French dressing or a mayonnaise dressing, as a rule, contains a sufficient proportion of some kind of oil to make the salad in which it is used somewhat high in fat. For the most part, salads do not contain carbohydrate in any quantity. If fruits are used, the salad will, of course, contain a certain amount of sugar. Salads in which potatoes, peas, beets, and other vegetables are used also contain starch or sugar in varying quantities. However, with the exception of potato salad, salads are probably never taken as a source of carbohydrate. In majority of salads, mineral salts are an important ingredient. Green-vegetable salads are the most valuable sources of mineral salts, and fruit salads come next. Vegetable and fruit salads serve to supply cellulose in the diet. Unless the meals contain sufficient cellulose in some other form, the use of such salads is an excellent way to introduce this material. Of course, the salads composed of foods high in cellulose are lower in food value than others, but the salad dressing usually helps to make up for this deficiency.

SALAD DRESSINGS

In addition to the ingredients used in the preparation of salads, dressings usually forms an important part. An accompaniment of some kind is generally served with salads to make them more attractive and more pleasing to the taste. When a salad is properly made, a salad dressing of some kind is usually added to the ingredients that are selected for the salad. Various salad dressings may be made to serve with salads. The kind of dressing to select depends both on the variety of salad served and on the personal preference of those to whom it is served. Some of these contain only a few ingredients and are comparatively simple to make, while others are complex and involve considerable work in their making. These vary greatly as to ingredients and consequently as to composition, but most of them contain considerable fat and therefore increase the food value of the salad. Sometimes these dressings contain no fat, and other times they have for their basis sweet or sour cream, but usually they are made so that they are somewhat acid to the taste. A number of recipes for salad dressings are included in this Ebook. See the subtitle "SALAD DRESSINGS AND THEIR PREPARATION" at the bottom.

SALAD MAKING

When the kind of salad to be served is decided on, the selection and preparation of the materials are the next matters to receive attention. Very often materials that are on hand are utilized in this way, but if it is possible to select the ingredients expressly for the salad, they should be very carefully chosen. Any kind of salad, but particularly a vegetable or a fruit salad, becomes much more attractive if it is made with ingredients that are in good condition and that are attractive in appearance. They should therefore be fresh and crisp and never mushy, wilted or limp. In the making of a salad, the cleaning of the ingredients used is a very important part of the work. While nothing should be wasted in the process of preparation, decayed or discolored leaves, stems, or parts of fruits and vegetables should, of course, be removed. Every lettuce leaf and every part of other salad vegetables should be looked over carefully and washed separately in cold water. To accomplish this, the stalks or leaves must be taken apart after the root is cut off. Then, before they are used, they should be examined carefully again in order to make sure that no small bugs nor worms and no dirt remain on them. It should be remembered that lettuce leaves bruise and break easily and so must be handled carefully if the best appearance is desired. After fruits and vegetables have been carefully cleaned, they are ready to be peeled and cut into pieces of the size desired for the salad. An effort should always be made to have the pieces equal in size, similar in shape, and not too small. They should be peeled in an economical way, but at the same time should be prepared as attractively as possible. When nuts are to be used in a salad, they should never be ground in a grinder; rather, they should be chopped or cut into small pieces with a knife. After being so prepared, they should be added to the salad just before it is put on the table. This is a matter that should not be overlooked, for if the salad is allowed to stand very long after the nuts are added they will discolor the dressing and cause the salad to become dark and gray looking.

SERVING SALADS

Several different ways of serving salads are in practice. Perhaps the most convenient method of serving this dish is to prepare individual portions of it on salad plates in the kitchen and then set these on the table at each person's place. If a simple table service is followed, the salad may be put on the table at the same time as the rest of the meal. The correct position for the salad plate is at the left-hand side of the dinner plate and just a little nearer to the edge of the table than the bread-and-butter plate. The plates on which salad is served should be large enough to prevent the difficulty in eating that would be experienced if the plate were a trifle small. It should therefore be remembered that the salad plate is the next larger in size to the bread and-butter plate. In case individual salads are to be prepared, the plate should first be garnished with whatever vegetable green is selected for this purpose. If lettuce is to be used, a single leaf, several very small center leaves, or a small quantity of shredded lettuce will be sufficient, for a great deal of garnish is never desirable. In case the leaves are very large, one may be divided in half and each part utilized. Then the salad ingredients, which have already been combined, should be piled in a neat heap on top of the garnish either with or without the salad dressing. If the salad dressing is not mixed with the materials, a spoonful or two of it should be placed on top of them. Another method of serving this dish is to place the entire salad on a rather large, deep plate, such as a chop plate or a regular salad dish, and then serve it at the table whenever it is desired. When this is done, the dish that is used should be well garnished with a bed of vegetable green in the same way that a small individual plate is garnished. Then the salad ingredients should be nicely arranged on this bed, and the dressing, if it has not already been mixed with them, should be poured over the whole. In serving salad in this way, there is much more chance of arranging the ingredients symmetrically and garnishing the salad attractively than when it is served on small plates. The large plate containing the salad, together with the small salad plates, should be placed before serving the salad. When it is served, a leaf of the lettuce or other green used for garnishing should first be put on each salad plate and the salad should be served on this. A large fork and a large spoon are needed when salad is served in this manner.

In a dinner, the salad is generally served as a separate course, but in such a meal as luncheon it may be used as the main dish. If it is used as a separate course, it should be served immediately after the dinner course has been removed from the table. The salad plate should be placed directly before the person served. Forks especially designed with a wide prong on one side and known as 'salad forks' are the right type of fork to serve with this dish, but if none are available ordinary table forks of a small size may be used. It should be remembered that the salad should not be cut with the knife at the table, but should be eaten entirely with the fork.

VARIETIES OF SALADS AND THEIR PREPARATION

VEGETABLE SALADS

With the knowledge already obtained of the food value of the vegetables that are generally used as ingredients in vegetable salads, the housewife ought to have no difficulty in determining whether she is giving her family a salad that is high or low in food value. For instance, she should know that the food value of a plain lettuce or cucumber salad is lower than that of one made from potatoes because of the different values in the vegetables used.

GREEN VEGETABLE SALAD.

There are a number of green vegetables that are much used for salad either alone or with other vegetables. All of them are used in practically the same way, but a point that should not be overlooked if an appetizing salad is desired is that they should always be fresh and crisp when served. Any salad dressing that is preferred may be served with them. Chief among these green vegetables come lettuce, including the ordinary leaf lettuce, head lettuce, and romaine lettuce, which is not so common as the other varieties. Several kinds of endive as well as watercress may also be used for salad.

MIXED VEGETABLE SALAD -1

One pint of cold boiled potatoes, cut in slices; one-third the quantity of cold boiled beets cut fine; one-third the quantity of green peas (winter beets and canned peas are as good as fresh ones); sprinkle with salt and pepper, then pour over it a French dressing made of a saltspoonful of salt, one of black pepper, a teaspoonful of onion juice or grated onion, three tablespoonfuls of olive oil and one of vinegar; mix thoroughly and set aside. When ready to serve spread over it a thick mayonnaise dressing and garnish with slices of beet, cut in shapes, hard boiled egg and parsley; if made in summer a border of crisp lettuce leaves is an additional garnish. If the quantity of vegetable is increased the amount of dressing must also be doubled or the salad will be dry.

MIX VEGETABLE SALAD -2

- 1 cup finely cut red cabbage
- 1 cup cold boiled beets
- 1 cup cold boiled carrots
- 1 cup cold boiled potatoes
- 1 cup chopped celery
- 1/2 cup pimentoes
- 1 head lettuce
- 1 cup French dressing

Soak cabbage in cold water 1 hour; drain and add beets, carrots and potatoes cut into small pieces; add celery. Mix well together, season with salt and pepper and serve on lettuce leaves. On top put strips of pimento and serve with French dressing, to which may be added one teaspoon onion juice.

CUCUMBER SALAD -1

Besides serving plain slices of cucumber on a lettuce leaf, as may be done at any time, cucumbers may be used as an ingredient in the making of many salads.

- 3 medium-sized cucumbers
- 1 c. diced tomato 1/2 c. diced celery
- Salad dressing
- Lettuce
- 1 pimiento

Peel the cucumbers, cut them into halves, and with a small spoon scoop out the cucumbers in chunks, so that a boat-shaped piece of cucumber that is about 1/4 inch thick remains. Dice the pieces of cucumber which have been scooped from the center, and place the cucumber shells in ice water so as to make them crisp. Mix the diced tomato, celery, and cucumber together, and just before serving drain them carefully so that no liquid remains. Mix with salad dressing, wipe the cucumber shells dry, fill them with the salad mixture, and place on salad plates garnished with lettuce leaves. Cut the pimiento into thin strips, and place three or four strips diagonally across the cucumber. Sufficient to Serve Six

CUCUMBER SALAD -2

Pare thickly, from end to end, and lay in ice-water one hour; wipe them, slice thin, and slice an onion equally thin. Strew salt over them, shake up a few times, cover and let remain in this brine for another hour. Then squeeze or press out every drop of water which has been extracted from the cucumbers. Put into a salad bowl, sprinkle with white pepper and scatter bits of parsley over them; add enough vinegar to cover. You may slice up an equal quantity of white or red radishes and mix with this salad.

CUCUMBER SALAD -3

Peel and slice a cucumber, mix together 1/2 a teaspoonful of salt, 1/4 of a teaspoonful of white pepper, and 2 tablespoonfuls of olive oil, stir it well together, then add very gradually 1 tablespoonful of vinegar, stirring it all the time. Put the sliced cucumber into a salad dish, and garnish it with nasturtium leaves and flowers.

CUCUMBER & TOMATO SALAD.

A salad made of cucumbers and tomatoes is very attractive because of the contrasting colors of the vegetables, and it is at the same time extremely palatable. When such a salad is to be made, small, firm tomatoes and rather large cucumbers that do not contain very large seeds should be selected. Peel the cucumbers and tomatoes and cut them into slices of any desired thickness. Garnish salad plates with lettuce, and on this place a ring of the slices, alternating the tomatoes with the cucumbers. In the center, put a slice of cucumber or tomato and serve with any desired salad dressing.

SLICED CUCUMBER & ONION SALAD.

An attractive way in which to serve sliced cucumbers and onions. A single large cucumber should be selected for this salad.

With a sharp knife, peel the skin from the cucumber in narrow strips back to the stem end, but do not cut the strips loose from the end. After the peeling has all been removed, place the cucumber on a board and cut it into thin slices. Place on a small platter, as shown, arrange slices of onion around the edge, and pour French dressing over the whole. Dust with paprika and serve. A number of slices of cucumber and one or two slices of onion should be served to each person.

ONION SALAD -1

To persons who are fond of the flavor of onions, the salad given in the accompanying recipe is very agreeable, but it is a wise plan not to serve onions or salads containing onions unless every one who is served is certain to enjoy them. When a salad is made from onions, a mild onion should be selected.

- 3 onions
- French dressing
- Parsley Lettuce

Peel the onions and slice them into thin slices. Chop the parsley and add it to 1 or 2 tablespoonfuls of French dressing. Use comparatively coarse leaves of lettuce and shred them. Arrange the slices of onion on a bed of the shredded lettuce, pour the French dressing with the parsley over all, and serve. Sufficient to Serve Six.

ONION SALAD -2

1 large boiled onion (Spanish), 3 large boiled potatoes, 1 teaspoonful of parsley, pepper and salt to taste, juice of 1 lemon, 2 or 3 tablespoonfuls of olive oil. Slice the onion and potatoes when quite cold, mix well together with the parsley and pepper and salt; add the lemon juice and oil, and mix well once more.

TOMATO SALAD -1

Fresh tomatoes make a delightful salad because of their appetizing appearance and color. In fact, when they are placed on a bed of green garnish, nothing can be more delightful. Tomatoes may be served whole on a lettuce leaf or they may be sliced. Then, again, they may be cut from the center into sections that are allowed to fall part way open. In any of these forms, they may be served with French dressing, mayonnaise, or any cooked salad dressing.

TOMATO SALAD -2

Six tomatoes, one-half cup of mayonnaise dressing, the crisp part of one head of lettuce. Peel the tomatoes and put them on the ice until they are very cold; make the mayonnaise and stand it on the ice until wanted; wash and dry the lettuce. When ready to serve, cut the tomatoes in halves, make twelve little nests with two or three salad leaves each, arrange on the dish, place half a tomato in each nest, put a tablespoonful of mayonnaise on each tomato and serve immediately.

TOMATO SALAD -3
(With Canned Tomatoes)

Rub through a coarse sieve one can of tomatoes; cover with cold water a half box of Cox gelatine and let it stand a half hour or more; then pour in enough hot water to thoroughly dissolve it; then mix with one full pint of the strained tomatoes; add a little salt; pour into small round moulds and put in a cool place to harden. Serve on lettuce leaves with mayonnaise dressing.

TOMATO SALAD -4

Select perfectly ripe tomatoes, and peel at least an hour before using. Slice, and place on ice or in a cool place. Serve plain or with lemon juice or sugar as preferred.

TOMATO SALAD -5

Use one half small yellow tomatoes and one half red. Slice evenly and lay in the dish in alternate layers. Powder lightly with sugar, and turn over them a cupful of orange juice to a pint of tomato, or if preferred, the juice of lemons may be used instead. Set on ice and cool before serving.

STUFFED TOMATO SALAD.

An attractive salad in which vegetables of almost any kind, fresh or canned, may be used to advantage is the stuffed tomato salad. Medium-sized, well-ripened tomatoes are best to select. The vegetables that may be used for the stuffing are celery, radishes, onions, cucumbers, cooked asparagus, green peas, and string beans. Any one or any desirable combination of these vegetables will make a satisfactory filling.

- 6 medium-sized tomatoes
- French dressing
- 1 1/2 c. diced vegetables
- Mayonnaise dressing

Salads and Salad Dressing Recipes

Cut out the stem and blossom ends of the tomatoes and hollow out the center so as to leave a shell. Dice the contents of the tomatoes and mix with the other diced vegetables. Marinate the diced vegetables with French dressing and put into the tomato shells, heaping each one as shown. Place on lettuce leaves and serve with mayonnaise.

TOMATO & STRING BEAN SALAD.

Besides being appetizing in flavor and appearance, tomato and string-bean salad has the advantage over some salads in that it can be made of either fresh or canned vegetables. For the salad here shown, tomatoes and beans canned by the cold-pack method were used. If it is desired to duplicate this salad, place a canned tomato or a peeled fresh tomato in the center of a plate garnished with lettuce and around it place several piles of three or four canned or freshly cooked beans. Serve with French dressing or any other desired salad dressing.

BEET SALAD -1

Cold boiled or baked beets, chopped quite fine, but not minced, make a nice salad when served with a dressing of lemon juice and whipped cream in the proportion of three tablespoonfuls of lemon juice to one half cup of whipped cream, and salt if desired.

BEET SALAD -2

Chop equal parts of boiled beets and fresh young cabbage. Mix thoroughly, add salt to taste, a few tablespoonfuls of sugar, and cover with diluted lemon juice. Equal quantities of cold boiled beets and cold boiled potatoes, chopped fine, thoroughly mixed, and served with a dressing of lemon juice and whipped cream, make a palatable salad.

BEET & BEAN SALAD.

An excellent winter salad and one that may be made from canned or left-over vegetables is beet & bean salad. If string beans happen to be left over or only part of a can remains, they may be combined with beets that are canned or freshly cooked for the purpose. This salad should be carefully combined just before serving.

- 1 c. string beans
- Lettuce
- 1 c. beets
- Salad dressing

Cut the string beans into half-inch lengths and cut the beets into half-inch dice. Season each well with salt and pepper. Just before serving, garnish salad plates with lettuce, combine the two vegetables, and place in a heap on a lettuce leaf. Pour French dressing or any other salad dressing desired over them, but do not mix the salad dressing with the vegetables. Sufficient to Serve Four.

BEET AND CAULIFLOWER SALAD

Take some thin slices of cooked beets, some cold cooked potatoes, some cold cooked cauliflower, and a little chopped parsley. Pour over the following dressing and add salt and pepper to taste:
Put one level teaspoon of mustard, one teaspoon anchovy sauce, one tablespoon of milk or cream, and one dessertspoon of vinegar. Mix the mustard with the anchovy, then add the milk, and lastly the vinegar.

STRING BEAN SALAD -1

Either string or wax beans may be used for string bean salad and they may be cooked freshly for the purpose or be home canned or commercially canned beans. To make this salad, place a neat pile of beans on a lettuce leaf resting on a plate and moisten with a few drops of vinegar or lemon juice. Serve with mayonnaise or cooked salad dressing. If desired, the beans may be cut into inch lengths and mixed with the dressing, but this does not make so attractive a salad.

STRING BEAN SALAD -2

String and remove the ends from one quart of beans. Cut into short lengths. Cover with boiling water, add one level tablespoon of wilt and cook until tender, but not soft. Drain and save one cup of the liquor. Cream one tablespoon of flour with two tablespoons of butter. Pour the liquid over the flour and butter, stirring constantly. Cook this sauce for five minutes, remove from stove and stir in two tablespoons of strained lemon juice. Pour this over the beans and serve.

STRING BEAN SALAD (FRENCH STYLE)

String the beans and boil them whole; when boiled tender and they have become cold, slice them lengthwise, cutting each bean into four long slices; season them an hour or two before serving, with a marinade of a little pepper, salt, and three spoonfuls of vinegar to one spoonful of oil. Just before serving, drain from them any drops of superfluous liquid that may have collected and carefully mix them with a French Salad dressing. This makes a delicious salad.

CABBAGE SALAD -1

A salad that always finds favor is made by combining cabbage with a boiled salad dressing or with an uncooked sour-cream dressing. To make cabbage salad, select a firm head of cabbage, pull off the outside leaves, and wash. Cut the head in half down through the heart and root and cut each half into quarters. place each quarter on a cutting board and with a sharp knife shave off the cabbage. If desired, however, the cabbage may be shredded with a cabbage cutter. If the cabbage, upon being cut, is found to be wilted, place it in cold water and let it stand until it becomes crisp. Drain off the water carefully and allow the cabbage to drip in a colander or dry it between pieces of old linen. With the cabbage thus prepared, season it with salt and mix it with the desired dressing. Serve on lettuce in a salad dish, on individual salad plates.

CABBAGE SALAD -2

Mix together one-half cup of sugar, one teaspoonful of mustard, one teaspoonful of salt, one- half teaspoonful black pepper; then add three well beaten eggs, one-half cup of vinegar, six tablespoonfuls of cream, three of butter. Cook the same as boiled custard in a kettle of water; when cold add the cabbage chopped fine.

CHOPPED CABBAGE SALAD

Take one pint of finely chopped cabbage; pour over it a dressing made of three tablespoonfuls of lemon juice, two tablespoonfuls of sugar, and a half cup of whipped cream, thoroughly beaten together in the order named; or serve with sugar and diluted lemon juice.

CABBAGE & CELERY SALAD.

Cabbage and celery combine very well, for they are similar in color and crispness. They can be procured at the same time of the year, and while celery is not cheap, cabbage is a comparatively inexpensive food and the two combined make an inexpensive salad. Because the color of both is very much the same, pimiento is added to give a contrasting color.

- 1 cup cabbage
- 1 cup celery
- 1 pimiento or green pepper
- 1/2 teaspoon. salt
- 2 Tablespoon. vinegar
- Lettuce
- Salad dressing

Select a firm head of cabbage, pull off the outside leaves, and wash. Cut the head in half down through the heart and root and cut each half into quarters. Cut the celery into thin pieces across the stem, and dice the green pepper or pimiento or both into very small dice. Measure each of these, combine them, season with the salt and vinegar, and just before serving drain carefully. Serve on lettuce with any desired salad dressing. Sufficient to Serve Four.

CARROT AND CABBAGE SALAD

- 1 medium-sized carrot
- 2 cupfuls cabbage
- 1/2 cupful roasted peanuts
- French or Cream Salad Dressing

Clean and scrape the carrot. Wash the cabbage. Put the carrot (uncooked), cabbage, and peanuts through the food chopper. Mix with French or Cream Salad Dressing. Add more seasoning if necessary. Serve at once.

BREAKFAST SALAD

- 2 Tomatoes
- 1 Cucumber
- 1 tablespoonful Oil
- 1 Spring Onion Half a Lettuce
- 2 tablespoonsful Vinegar

Scald the tomatoes and take off the skin, and put them into cold water or on to the ice until quite cold. Cut them up the same as an orange; peel and cut up the cucumber into very thin slices and mince up the onion. Sprinkle these with pepper and salt, pour over the oil and vinegar. Shred up the lettuce and lay on the top, it is then ready to serve.

WINTER SALAD -1

A salad made entirely of winter vegetables may be prepared when there are no fresh vegetables in supply. If any of the vegetables are left over, the others may be prepared to use with the left-over ones. A good plan to follow when carrots, turnips, or potatoes are being prepared for a meal is to cook more than is necessary for the one meal and then set aside part of them for a salad to be served at another meal.

- 1 cup turnips, diced
- 1 cup carrots, diced
- 1 cup. potatoes, diced
- 1 Tb. chopped onion
- French dressing
- Lettuce
- Salad dressing

Cook turnips, carrots, and potatoes whole in boiling water until tender enough to be pierced with a fork. If they have not been peeled before cooking, peel and cut into small dice. Mix, add the onion, marinate with French dressing, and allow to stand for a short time. Garnish salad plates with lettuce leaves, pile the salad on the lettuce, and serve with any desired salad dressing. Sufficient to Serve Six.

WINTER SALAD -2

INGREDIENTS: Endive, mustard-and-cress, boiled beetroot, 3 or 4 hard-boiled eggs, celery.

The above ingredients form the principal constituents of a winter salad, and may be converted into a very pretty dish, by nicely contrasting the various colours, and by tastefully garnishing it. Shred the celery into thin pieces, after having carefully washed and cut away all wormeaten pieces; cleanse the endive and mustard and cress free from grit, and arrange these high in the centre of a salad-bowl or dish; garnish with the hard-boiled eggs and beetroot, both of which should be cut in slices; and pour into the dish, but not over the salad.

SUMMER SALAD.

INGREDIENTS: 3 lettuces, 2 handfuls of mustard-and-cress, 10 young radishes, a few slices of cucumber.

Let the herbs be as fresh as possible for a salad, and, if at all stale or dead-looking, let them lie in water for an hour or two, which will very much refresh them. Wash and carefully pick them over, remove any decayed or wormeaten leaves, and drain them thoroughly by swinging them gently in a clean cloth. With a knife, cut the lettuces into small pieces, and the radishes and cucumbers into thin slices; arrange all these ingredients lightly on a dish, with the mustard and cress, and pour under, but not over the salad. Add souce as necessary. Do not stir it up until it is to be eaten. It may be garnished with hard-boiled eggs, cut in slices, sliced cucumbers, nasturtiums, cut vegetable-flowers, and many other things that taste will always suggest to make a pretty and elegant dish. In making a good salad, care must be taken to have the herbs freshly gathered, and thoroughly drained before the sauce is added to them, or it will be watery and thin.

CAULIFLOWER SALAD -1

Cauliflower makes a rather unusual salad, and for a change it will be found to be delightful. It does not combine with other vegetables very readily, but a cooked floweret or two may often be used to garnish another vegetable salad.

- Cauliflower
- Lettuce
- Salad dressing

Prepare a head of cauliflower for cooking as usual. Then cook in boiling salted water until tender, but quite firm. Drain and cool. Arrange the flowerets on a salad plate garnished with lettuce and serve with French dressing or any other desired salad dressing. Sufficient to Serve Six.

CAULIFLOWER SALAD -2

- 1 Cauliflower
- Half a Lettuce
- 2 Eggs
- 1/2 gill Oil and Vinegar

Boil the cauliflower by directions given elsewhere and branch it carefully. Boil the eggs hard, separate the whites from the yolks; chop the whites small and cut the yolks in slices. Shred up the lettuce in a bowl and put the branches of cauliflower all round it, and the slices of yolk of egg outside as a border. Pour on the salad dressing and put the white of egg in little heaps on the lettuce. It is then ready to serve.

CAULIFLOWER & TOMATO SALAD.

A salad in which cauliflower and tomatoes are combined is attractive in appearance if it is nicely made. It also has the advantage of being simple to prepare. When cauliflower is cooked for salad, care must be taken not to cook it so long as to discolor it or cause it to fall to pieces..

- 3 tomatoes
- Lettuce
- 6 cauliflower flowerets
- Dressing

Select firm, ripe, medium-sized tomatoes. Place them in boiling water to scald them, and then dip them quickly into cold water and remove the skins. Cut out the stem ends and slice each tomato half way between the stem and blossom ends. Place each half tomato on a salad plate garnished with a lettuce leaf, stick a stem of the cauliflower into the center, and serve with boiled salad dressing or mayonnaise. Sufficient to Serve Six.

CELERY SALAD -1

One means of using stalks of celery that are just a little too coarse to serve nicely on the table is to combine them with radishes and make a salad. The more tender celery, of course, makes a better salad. If the radishes selected for the salad are of the red variety and they are used without peeling, they add a touch of color to the dish.

- 1-1/2 c. diced celery
- 1/2 c. diced radishes 2 Tb. chopped onion
- Salad dressing
- Lettuce

Cut the celery into fine dice, and dice the radishes more finely than the celery. Mix the two together, add the onion, and just before serving mix with any desired salad dressing. Serve on salad plates garnished with lettuce. Sufficient to Serve Five.

CELERY SALAD -2

- 1 Head of Celery
- 1 Lettuce
- Salad Dressing

Pull the celery to pieces, wash it, and cut into small pieces; shred up some lettuce and lay it at the bottom the dish. Stir the celery into the dressing and lay it on the top of the lettuce. Cover with more lettuce, and serve.

BOILED CELERY ROOT SALAD

Pare and wash the celery roots (they should be the size of large potatoes), put on to boil in a little salted water, and when tender remove from the water and set away until cool. Cut in slices about an eighth of an inch thick; sprinkle each slice with fine salt, sugar and white pepper; pour enough white wine vinegar over the salad to cover. A few large raisins boiled will add to the appearance of this salad. Serve cold in a salad bowl, lined with fresh lettuce leaves.

PEAS & CELERY SALAD.

Peas may be freshly cooked for this salad, but canned peas will do just as well. Left-over peas not prepared with cream sauce may also be utilized nicely in this way, or if a portion of a can of peas is needed for the meal, the remainder may be used for a smaller quantity of salad than here stated. Boiled salad dressing will be found to be best for this combination of vegetables.

- 1 c. peas
- Boiled salad dressing
- 1 c. diced celery
- Lettuce

Drain canned peas as dry as possible and mix with the diced celery. Just before serving, add the salad dressing and mix thoroughly. Serve on salad plates garnished with lettuce.

POTATO SALAD -1

Potato salad is usually considered to be an economical salad. It may be made with left-over potatoes or potatoes cooked especially for this purpose. If there are in supply a large number of small potatoes, which are difficult to use in ordinary ways, they may be cooked with the skins on and peeled to be used for salad when they have cooled. A boiled salad dressing is perhaps the most desirable for such a salad.

Cut into dice six medium sized potatoes boiled); three medium onions; salt and pepper them to taste; pour over and mix well the following dressing:

Three well beaten eggs, three large tablespoonfuls of strong vinegar, a lump of butter size of a walnut, pinch of salt, pepper and mustard (unmixed); put on the stove and cook to a thin custard, stirring constantly. For serving four to six people.

POTATO SALAD -2

- 2 c. diced potatoes
- Salt
- 1 medium-sized onion Boiled salad dressing
- 1/2 tsp. celery seed
- Lettuce
- 1 Tb. parsley, chopped
- 1 hard-cooked egg

Dice the potatoes into 1/2-inch dice, chop the onion fine, and mix the two. Add the celery seed and parsley and season the whole with salt. Just before serving, mix well with boiled dressing. Garnish a salad bowl or salad plates with lettuce, place the salad on the lettuce, and then garnish with slices of hard cooked egg. Sufficient to Serve Four.

POTATO SALAD -3

INGREDIENTS: 10 or 12 cold boiled potatoes, 4 tablespoonfuls of tarragon or plain vinegar, 6 tablespoonfuls of salad-oil, pepper and salt to taste, 1 teaspoonful of minced parsley.

Cut the potatoes into slices about 1/2 inch in thickness; put these into a salad-bowl with oil and vinegar in the above proportion; season with pepper, salt, and a teaspoonful of minced parsley; stir the salad well, that all the ingredients may be thoroughly incorporated, and it is ready to serve. This should be made two or three hours before it is wanted for table. Anchovies, olives, or pickles may be added to this salad, as also slices of cold beef, fowl, or turkey.

POTATO SALAD -4

Slice up some cold boiled potatoes. Sprinkle with salt, pepper, and chopped parsley. Mix the oil and vinegar together in the proportion of two of oil to one of vinegar; pour this over, let it stand for an hour, and serve.

POTATO SALAD -5

- 1 1/2 c. diced potatoes
- Salt
- 1/2 c. diced cucumber Boiled salad dressing
- 1/2 c. diced celery
- Lettuce
- 1 medium-sized onion

Prepare the vegetables in the usual way, dicing them carefully, and just before serving mix them together, season well with salt, and add the salad dressing. Boiled dressing is preferable. Place in a salad bowl or on salad plates garnished with lettuce.

GREEN SALAD

Imported or domestic endive, chicory, escarole and Romaine or lettuce must be washed, made crisp in cold water, and dried in a bag on the ice. Serve them with French dressing. Imported endive may, however, be served with mayonnaise, if desired.

LETTUCE SALAD -1

The French style of making lettuce salad is as follows: After dressing the salad, mix it in one tablespoon of oil, then take only two tablespoons of white wine vinegar, mixed with a very little pepper and salt, and just turn the lettuce over and over in this mixture.

LETTUCE SALAD -2

- 2 Lettuces
- 1 tablespoonful Condensed Milk
- 2 teaspoonful Mustard
- 2 Eggs
- 1/2 gill Vinegar
- 1/4 gill Oil
- Pepper and Salt

Boil the eggs hard; take the yolk of one and put it into a basin and work it quite smooth with a spoon. Then add the mustard made with vinegar instead of water, the condensed milk, pepper, and salt, and then the oil slowly; last of all the vinegar. Mix it all very thoroughly. Cut off the outside leaves of the lettuce, and pull it all to pieces, wash in cold water and dry thoroughly in a cloth. Break into small pieces and put into a salad bowl, pour over the dressing. Garnish with the other egg and the white that was not used in the dressing. These should be cut into slices and placed round. A few of the best pieces of lettuce should be laid over the dressing.

CHIFFONADE SALAD

Lettuce, dandelion, chicory, a little chopped beet, chopped celery, a bit of tomato are mixed and covered with French dressing. The dressing is usually flavored both with onion and garlic.

ASPARAGUS SALAD -1

Boil the asparagus in salted water, being very careful not to break the caps; drain, and pour over it when cold a mayonnaise dressing, with some chopped parsley. Serve each person with three or four stems on a plate, with a little mayonnaise dressing. Do not use a fork; take the stems in the fingers and dip in the dressing.

ASPARAGUS SALAD -2

Salad in which asparagus is the chief ingredient is one that may be served during the entire year, for either freshly cooked or canned asparagus may be used; in fact, the canned asparagus is considered by many persons to be better than that which is freshly cooked.

- Lettuce
- 1 pimiento
- 1 can asparagus
- Salad dressing

Garnish salad plates with the lettuce. Place the asparagus tips in an orderly pile on the lettuce leaf. Cut a thin strip of the pimiento, and place this across the tips in the center. Just before serving, pour a spoonful or two of any desired salad dressing over this or place the salad on the table and serve the dressing, allowing each person to take what is desired. Sufficient to Serve Five.

BEETROOT AND MACARONI SALAD

- 3 oz. Macaroni
- 2 tablespoonsful Oil
- 1 bunch Beetroot
- Pepper and Salt
- 2 tablespoonful Vinegar

Boil both the macaroni and the beetroot by directions given elsewhere. When quite cold, peel and slice up the beetroot and cut the macaroni into pieces about two inches long; arrange them in alternate layers on a dish. Blend the oil and vinegar with the salt and pepper and pour it over; let it stand for an hour, basting continually with the oil and vinegar. By that time it should be of a bright red colour. It is then ready to serve.

TURNIP SALAD

4 Young Turnips
2 Spring Onions
2 Boiled Potatoes
Half a Lettuce Salad Dressing

Peel and slice up the turnips and boil them for twenty minutes, or until soft. Let them get quite cold. Shred up very small the onions, and slice up the potatoes. Break up half a lettuce. Arrange these neatly in a bowl and pour over a simple salad dressing or remoulade sauce.

ENDIVE SALAD

Take a head of endive, wash it and dry it well, and put it into a salad-bowl. Pour over it three tablespoons of good olive-oil. Mix one tablespoon of honey (or sugar), one of vinegar, and salt and pepper in a cup, and pour over the salad just before serving.

ITALIAN VEGITABLE SALAD

Cut one carrot and one turnip into slices, and cook them in boiling soup. When cold, mix them with two cold boiled potatoes and one beet cut into strips. Add a very little chopped leeks or onion, pour some sauce over the salad, and garnish with watercress.

ALLA POLLASTRA SALAD

Chop up six lettuce-leaves and three stalks of celery, cut up the remains of a cold fowl in small pieces, and mix with one tablespoon of vinegar and salt and pepper in a salad bowl. Pour a cup of mayonnaise sauce over, and garnish with quarters of hard-boiled egg, one tablespoon of capers, six stoned olives, and some small, tender lettuce-leaves.

ALLA MACEDOINE SALAD

Cut into small pieces one cold boiled beet and half an onion. Add some cold boiled string-beans, some cold boiled asparagus tips, two tablespoons of cold cooked peas, one cold boiled carrot, and some celery. Mix them together, and pour over all a mayonnaise sauce. Add the juice of a lemon and serve.

HUNGARIAN VEGETABLE SALAD

Mix together one cup each of cold cooked peas, beans, carrots, and potatoes. Cover with French dressing and let stand for twenty minutes. Add one cup of smoked salmon or haddock, cut in small pieces, the chopped whites of four hard-boiled eggs and two stalks of celery. Mix thoroughly, garnish top with yolk of egg pressed through a wire sieve; and with cucumbers and beets, cut in fancy shapes.

FRUIT SALADS

Salads made of fruit are undoubtedly the most delicious that can be prepared. In addition to being delightful in both appearance and flavor, they afford another means of introducing fruit into the diet. As fruit is decidedly beneficial for all persons with a normal digestion, every opportunity to include it in the diet should be grasped. Some fruit salads are comparatively bland in flavor while others are much more acid, but the mild ones are neither so appetizing nor so beneficial as those which are somewhat tart. Advantage should be taken of the various kinds of fresh fruits during the seasons when they can be obtained, for usually very appetizing salads can be made of them. However, the family need not be deprived of fruit salads during the winter when fresh fruits cannot be secured, for delicious salads can be made from canned and dried fruits, as well as from bananas and citrus fruits, which are usually found in all markets.

FRUIT SALAD DRESSING

Various dressings may be served with fruit salad, and usually the one selected depends on the preference of those to whom it is served. However, an excellent dressing for salad of this kind and one that most persons find delicious is made from fruit juices thickened by means of eggs. Whenever a recipe in this Section calls for a fruit salad dressing, this is the one that is intended.

- 1/2 c. pineapple, peach, or pear juice
- 1/2 c. orange juice 1/4 c. lemon juice
- 1/4 c. sugar
- 2 eggs

Mix the fruit juices, add the sugar, beat the eggs slightly, and add them. Put the whole into a double boiler and cook until the mixture begins to thicken. Remove from the fire and beat for a few seconds with a rotary egg beater. Cool and serve.

Mixed FRUIT SALAD -1

The combination of fruits given in the accompanying recipe makes a very good salad, but it need not be adhered to strictly. If one or more of the fruits is not in supply, it may be omitted and some other used. In case canned pineapple is used for the salad, the juice from the fruit may be utilized in making a fruit salad dressing.

- 1 grapefruit
- 2 oranges
- 1 banana
- 2 apples
- 2 slices pineapple
- Salad dressing
- Lettuce

Prepare the grapefruit and oranges according to the directions previously given. Slice the banana crosswise into 1/4-inch slices and cut each slice into four sections. Dice the apples and cut the pineapple in narrow wedge-shaped pieces. Mix the fruit just before serving. Add the salad dressing, which may be fruit-salad dressing, French dressing, or some other desirable salad dressing, by mixing it with the fruit or merely pouring it over the top. Serve on salad plates garnished with lettuce leaves. Place a maraschino cherry on top. Sufficient to Serve Six.

MIXED FRUIT SALAD -2

Take sweet, ripe oranges, apples, bananas, and grapes. Peel the oranges, quarter them, and remove skin and pips. Peel and core the apples and cut into thin slices. Wash and dry the grapes, and remove from stalks. Skin and slice the bananas. Put the prepared fruit into a glass dish in alternate layers. Squeeze the juice from 2 sweet oranges and pour over the salad. Any other fresh fruit in season may be used for this salad. Castor sugar may be sprinkled over if desired, and cream used in place of the juice. Grated nuts are also a welcome addition.

MIXED FRUIT SALAD -3

Slice one pineapple, three oranges, and three bananas. Pour over it a French mayonnaise, put on lettuce leaves and serve at once. For those who do not care for the mayonnaise, make a syrup of one cup of sugar and one-half cup of water, boil until thick, add juice of lemon, let slightly cool, then pour over fruit. Let stand on ice for one hour. Another nice dressing is one cup of claret, one-half cup of sugar, and piece of lemon. Always use lemon juice in preference to vinegar in fruit salads. All fruits that go well together may be mixed. This is served just before desert.

FRUIT SALAD (ICED)

Make one quart of lemon or orange water ice and stand it aside for at least one or two hours to ripen. Make a fruit salad from stemmed strawberries, sliced bananas cut into tiny bits, a few very ripe cherries, a grated pineapple if you have it, and the pulp of four or five oranges. After the water ice is frozen rather hard, pack it in a border mold, put on the lid or cover and bind the seam with a strip of muslin dipped in paraffin or suet, and repack to freeze for three or four hours. Sweeten the fruit combination, if you like, add a tablespoonful or two of brandy and sherry, and stand this on the ice until very cold. At serving time, turn the mold of water ice on to a round compote dish, quickly fill the centre with fruit salad, garnish the outside with fresh roses or violets, and send at once to the table.

FRUIT AND NUT SALAD

Slice two bananas, two oranges and mix them with one-half cup of English walnuts and the juice of one-half lemon with French dressing. Serve on lettuce leaves.

HUNGARIAN FRUIT SALAD

Mix together equal parts of banana, orange, pineapple, grapefruit and one-half cup of chopped nuts. Marinate with French dressing. Fill apple or orange skins with mixture. Arrange on a bed of watercress or lettuce leaves. Sprinkle with paprika.

RUSSIAN FRUIT SALAD

Peel and pit some peaches, cut in slices and add as much sliced pineapple, some apricots, strawberries and raspberries, put these in a dish. Prepare a syrup of juice of two lemons, two oranges, one cup of water and one pound sugar, a half teaspoon of powdered cinnamon and grated rind of lemon. Boil this syrup for five minutes, then pour over the fruit, tossing the fruit from time to time until cool. Place on ice and serve cold.

SUMMER MIX FRUIT SALAD.

Any agreeable combination of fruits which may be obtained during the same season will be suitable for summer mix salad. The combination given in the accompanying recipe includes strawberries, pineapple, and cherries. However, pineapple and cherries may be used alone, or strawberries and pineapple may be used without the cherries, or red raspberries may be used to garnish such a salad.

- 3/4 c. strawberries, cut into halves
- 3/4 c. pineapple, cut into dice 3/4 c. sweet cherries, seeded
- Lettuce
- Fruit-salad dressing

Prepare the fruits just before serving. Put them together, place on salad plates garnished with lettuce, and serve with the fruit-salad dressing.

FILBERT & CHERRY SALAD.

If something different in the way of salad is desired, cherries that have been seeded and then filled with filberts will prove a delightful change. With this salad, any salad dressing may be served, but fruit-salad dressing makes it especially delicious.

DATE & WALNUT SALAD.

Persons who are fond of dates will find a salad made of dates and walnuts very palatable. In addition, such a salad is high in food value. Select firm whole dates, wash, and dry between clean towels. Cut a slit in the side of each date and remove the seed. Place half an walnut meat inside and press the date together. Garnish salad plates with lettuce and serve five or six of the dates in a star shape for each serving. In the center, pour a spoonful or two of cream salad dressing, boiled salad dressing, or any other dressing that may be desired.

APPLE AND NUT SALAD

- 4 tart apples
- 1 cupful of pecan meats
- 24 blanched almonds
- 2 sweet Spanish peppers
- The rule for French dressing

Peel the apples, cut them into dice, squeeze over the juice of one or two lemons, and stand them aside until wanted. The lemon juice will prevent discoloration. Chop the nuts. At serving time line the salad bowl with a layer of chopped celery or cabbage or lettuce leaves, then a layer of apples, nuts, celery, apples and nuts. Baste with the French dressing, and, if you have them, garnish with the sweet peppers cut into strips, and use at once.

APPLE, DATE & ORANGE SALAD.

The combination of fruits required by the accompanying recipe is an easy one to procure in the winter time. Apple and date salad is a combination much liked, but unless it is served with a rather sour dressing, it is found to be too bland and sweet for most persons. The addition of the orange gives just the acid touch that is necessary to relieve this monotonous sweetness.

- 1 c. diced apples Lettuce
- 3/4 c. dates, seeded Salad dressing
- 2 oranges
- Lettuce
- Salad Dressing

Peel the apples and dice them into fine pieces. Wash the dates, remove the seeds, and cut each date into six or eight pieces. Prepare the oranges as directed for preparing oranges for salad, and cut each section into two or three pieces. Just before serving, mix the fruits carefully so as not to make the salad look mushy, pile in a neat heap on garnished salad plates, and serve with any desired dressing. Sufficient to Serve Six

Salads and Salad Dressing Recipes

ORANGE SALAD.

INGREDIENTS: 6 oranges, 1/4 lb. of muscatel raisins, 2 oz. of pounded sugar, 4 tablespoonfuls of any juice you like. You get to choose the flavor you like by the juice that you choose..

Peel 5 of the oranges; divide them into slices without breaking the pulp, and arrange them on a glass dish. Stone the raisins, mix them with the sugar and juice, and mingle them with the oranges. Squeeze the juice of the other orange over the whole, and the dish is ready for table. A little pounded spice may be put in when the flavour is liked; but this ingredient must be added very sparingly.

CALIFORNIA SALAD.

During the months in which California grapes can be found in the market, a very delicious salad can be made by combining them with grapefruit and oranges. Either Malaga or Tokay grapes ma y b e u s ed .

- 1-1/2 c. grapes
- 2 oranges Salad
- 1 grapefruit
- Lettuce
- Salad Dressing

Prepare the grapes by washing them in cold water, cutting them into halves, and removing the seeds. Remove the sections from the oranges and grapefruit in the way previously directed, and cut each section into three or four pieces. Mix the fruits and drain carefully so that they contain no juice or liquid. Pile in a heap on salad plates garnished with lettuce and serve with any desired dressing.

APPLE & CELERY SALAD.

If an excellent winter salad is desired, apple and celery salad should be selected, for both celery and apples are best during the winter months. As they are very similar in color, they are not especially appetizing in appearance when combined for a salad, but they make a very popular combination with most persons.

- 1 c. diced apples
- Boiled salad dressing
- 1 c. diced celery
- Lettuce

Prepare the apples and celery as short a time before serving as possible, but if it is necessary that the apples stand for any length of time, sprinkle them with a little lemon juice and water to keep them from turning brown. Just before serving, mix them with the salad dressing. Place on salad plates garnished with lettuce and serve. Sufficient to Serve Four.

WALDORF SALAD.

- 1 c. diced apples
- Boiled salad dressing
- 1 c. diced celery
- Lettuce
- 1/2 c. chopped English walnut meats.

Prepare the apples and celery as short a time before serving as possible, but if it is necessary that the apples stand for any length of time, sprinkle them with a little lemon juice and water to keep them from turning brown. Add 1/2 cupful of chopped walnut meats is added, what is known as Waldorf salad will result. The nuts, which should be added to the mixture just before placing it on the table. Nuts that are to be used for such a purpose should not be run through a grinder, but should be cut with a knife or chopped with a chopping knife and bowl. Just before serving, mix them with the salad dressing. Place on salad plates garnished with lettuce and serve.

GRAPEFRUIT & CELERY SALAD.

Celery is sometimes used with grapefruit to make a salad. This combination is most often served with French dressing, but any other desirable dressing may be used as well. Prepare the grapefruit in the same way as oranges are prepared for salad, and cut each section into three or four pieces. Add to this an equal amount of diced celery and serve on a lettuce leaf with any desired dressing.

BANANA SALAD -1

Peel and scrape bananas. Place them on lettuce leaves or surround with a border of shredded lettuce. Cover with Cream Salad or Mayonnaise Dressing and sprinkle chopped peanuts or California walnuts over them. Serve at once.

Banana Salad may be varied by serving it with Cream Salad Dressing to which peanut butter is added,(1/2 cupful salad dressing and 1/4 cupful peanut butter). Do not use the chopped peanuts with this combination. A mixture of sliced apples and bananas served with the peanut butter dressing makes a pleasing salad.

BANANA SALAD -2

For this use the red bananas. Roll them out of the skin rather than strip the skin from them, and cut them into slices a half inch thick. Cover the bottom of your salad bowl with crisp lettuce leaves, then put over the bananas, allowing one banana to each two persons. Squeeze over the juice of a lemon, and, when ready to serve, baste with French dressing.

BANANA & PEANUT SALAD.

A very good fruit-and-nut combination for a salad consists of bananas and ground peanuts. The bananas, after being cut in half lengthwise, are rolled in the peanuts, placed on a lettuce leaf, and served with dressing. If it is desired to improve the flavor, the bananas may be dipped into the salad dressing before being rolled in the peanuts.

Peel the required number of bananas, scrape the pithy material from their surface, and cut in half lengthwise. Grind the peanuts rather fine and roll each half of banana in them. Place on a garnished salad plate and serve with boiled dressing.

BANANA AND ORANGE SALAD

Peel and slice up some ripe bananas and oranges, removing the pips from the oranges, but saving the juice. Take a deep glass dish, lay at the bottom some bananas, then a layer of oranges. Sprinkle well with sugar, then some more bananas and oranges and sugar, until all the materials are used up. Cover and let it stand for an hour, then serve as a sweet.

COSMOPOLITAN SALAD

Take any fruits in season, such as oranges, mandarins, passion fruit, apricots, nectarines, pineapples, bananas, etc. Peel and slice them up, and put them into a glass dish in layers, with plenty of sugar between each layer. Stand in a cool place for an hour covered over, and it is ready to serve.

FRUIT IN CANTALOUPE SHELLS.

During cantaloupe season, a delightful fruit salad can be made by combining several different kinds of fruit with the meat of cantaloupe and serving the mixture in the cantaloupe shells. Such a salad is an excellent one to serve when dainty refreshments are desired or when something unusual is wanted for a nice luncheon.

Cut cantaloupes in half crosswise, and, using the French cutter, cut some of the meat into round balls. Dice the remainder and mix with any combination of fruit desired. Place this in the cantaloupe shells after cutting points in the top edge. Garnish with the balls cut from the cantaloupe and serve with any desired dressing.

PINEAPPLE & NUT SALAD.

Because of its refreshing flavor, pineapple makes a delicious salad. It may be combined with various foods, but is very good when merely nuts and salad dressing are used.

Place slices of canned pineapple on salad plates garnished with lettuce leaves. Mix whipped cream with salad dressing until the dressing becomes stiff, and place a spoonful or two of this in the center of each slice of pineapple. Sprinkle generously with chopped nuts, English walnuts or pecans being preferable.

MARSHMALLOW SALAD

Cut up one-quarter pound of marshmallows into small squares, also contents of one-half can of pineapple. Let the marshmallows be mixed with the pineapples quite a while before salad is put together; add to this one-quarter pound of shelled pecans. Make a drip mayonnaise of one yolk of egg into which one-half cup of oil is stirred drop by drop; cut this with lemon juice, but do not use any sugar; to two tablespoons of mayonnaise, add four tablespoons of whipped cream. Serve on fresh, green lettuce-leaves.

HIGH PROTEIN SALADS

Salads that are made with cheese, eggs, fish, or meat may be classed as High Protein Salads, for, as has already been learned, these foods are characterized by the protein they contain. Of course, those made almost entirely of meat or fish are higher in this food substance than the others. However, the salads that contain a combination of cheese and fruit are comparatively high in protein, and at the same time they supply to the diet what is desirable in the way of a fruit salad.

EGG SALAD

- 6 Eggs
- 1 Lettuce
- 1 bunch Watercress
- Mayonnaise or Salad Dressing
- 1 Beet root

Put the eggs into boiling water and boil fifteen minutes. Plunge into cold water till quite cold, peel and cut into quarters. Wash and cleanse the watercress and lettuce and cut into pieces. Put a layer of this at the bottom of the bowl, then one of eggs dipped in the dressing, then another of lettuce and egg until all are used up, leaving plenty of lettuce for the top. Garnish with sprigs of watercress and slices of beetroot alternately.

EGGPLANT SALAD (TURKISH STYLE)

Use small eggplants. Place on end of toasting fork under broiler gas flame until the peel is black; remove the skin. The eggplant will then be tender; chop with wooden spoon, add lemon juice, parsley chopped fine, and olive oil.

EGG SALAD WITH MAYONNAISE.

1 lb. of cold boiled potatoes, 6 hard-boiled eggs, the juice of 1/2 a lemon, pepper and salt to taste. Cut the potatoes and eggs into slices, dust them with pepper and salt, add the lemon juice, and mix all well together. Cover with mayonnaise and garnish with watercress.

CHEESE SALAD.

Put some finely shredded lettuce in a glass dish, and over this put some young sliced onions, some mustard and cress, a layer of sliced tomatoes, and two hard-boiled eggs, also sliced. Add salt and pepper, and then over all put a nice layer of grated cheese. Serve with a dressing composed of equal parts of cream, salad oil, and vinegar, into which had been smoothly mixed a little mustard .

PEACH & CREAM CHEESE SALAD.

An excellent way of using canned peaches is to combine them with cream cheese for a salad. If a smaller salad is desired, half a peach may be used and the cheese placed on top of it. Firm yellow peaches are the best ones to use for this dish.

- Lettuce
- Salad dressing
- 8 halves of pecans or walnuts
- 2 Tb. cream 1/4 tsp. salt
- 1 pkg. Cream cheese
- 8 halves canned peaches

Mix the cream and salt with the cheese and shape into balls. Place a ball between two peach halves, and press them together tightly. Place on garnished salad plates, pour salad dressing over the top, and garnish with two halves of the nuts. If desired, the nuts may be chopped and sprinkled over the top. Sufficient to Serve Four.

PEAR & CHEESE SALAD.

- 2 Tb. cream
- Lettuce
- 1/4 tsp. salt
- 4 halves English walnuts
- 1 pkg. cream cheese
- Salad dressing
- 8 halves canned pears

Mix the cream and salt with the cheese and shape into balls. Place one-half of a pear with the hollow side up on a salad plate garnished with a lettuce leaf and the other half with the hollow side down beside it. Put a ball of the cheese in the hollow of the upturned half and press half an English walnut on top of that. Add the dressing and serve. French dressing is recommended for this salad.

MACARONI & CHEESE SALAD

- 1/4 lb. Macaroni
- 1/4 lb. Cheese
- 1 teaspoonful French Mustard
- 3 tablespoonsful Oil
- 3 table spoonsful Vinegar
- 1/2 Head of Celery
- 1/2 Lettuce

Boil the macaroni, or use any cold that may be in the larder. Cut it into pieces about three inches long, cut the cheese into very thin slices, and cut the celery into very small pieces. Lay these alternately in a bowl with some shredded lettuce. Make a dressing of the mustard, oil, and vinegar, and pour it over. Garnish with a little beetroot, and serve.

Green Pepper & Cheese Salad.

Vegetable and cheese combination in the form of a salad can be made of green pepper and cheese. To make this kind of salad, select firm green peppers, one being sufficient if a large one can be obtained. Season cream cheese well with paprika and a little additional salt if necessary. Cut the top from the pepper, clean out the inside, and pack tight with the cheese. Cut the filled pepper into thin slices, place two or three of these slices on a salad plate garnished with lettuce leaves, and serve with French dressing.

PEPPER & CHEESE SALAD

Fill green peppers with a mixture of cream cheese and chopped olives. Set on the ice and then slice the peppers and serve a slice (shaped like a four-leaf clover) on a leaf of lettuce. Small brown bread sandwiches go well with this.

DAISY SALAD.

This salad resembles a daisy. To make it, cut celery into strips about 2 inches long and trim one end of each round. These strips will serve to represent the daisy petals. Place them on salad plates garnished with lettuce, laying them so that they radiate from the center and their round ends are toward the outside of the plate. Then, for the center of the daisy effect, cut the yolks of hard-cooked eggs into halves and place one half, with the rounded side up, on the ends of the celery. Serve with French dressing.

HUMPTY DUMPTY SALAD.

Humpty Dumpty salad is very attractive and extremely appetizing. It consists of tomatoes and hard-cooked eggs garnished with pieces of stuffed olives, the manner in which the egg is placed in each portion accounting for its name.

For this salad, select rather small, firm, ripe tomatoes. Peel them in the usual way, and when cutting out the stem remove a sufficient portion of the tomato to accommodate the end of an egg. Place each tomato with this part uppermost on a salad plate garnished with lettuce. Cut the hard-cooked eggs into halves, crosswise, remove the yolk and mash and season it with salt, pepper, and a little vinegar. Replace the yolk in the white and force this into the depression in the tomato. Place a stuffed olive in the egg yolk and serve with French or other desired salad dressing.

WATER-LILY SALAD.

A means of using eggs in salad without the addition of other foods is found in water-lily salad. If eggs are to be served for a luncheon or some other light meal, this method may add a little variety to the usual ways of serving them.

Hard-cook one egg for each person to be served, remove the shells, and cut the eggs into halves, lengthwise. Remove the yolks, mash them, and season with salt, pepper, and vinegar. Cut the halves of egg whites into three or four pointed pieces, cutting from end to end of the half. Place these in a star shape on salad plates garnished with lettuce. Form the seasoned egg yolk into a ball and place it in the center over the ends of the egg whites. Serve with any desired salad dressing.

EASTER SALAD.

Cream cheese makes an attractive salad when formed into egg-shaped balls and served in a nest of shredded lettuce. To prepare this salad, which is known as Easter salad, shred lettuce finely and place it in the shape of a nest on salad plates. Make tiny egg-shaped balls of cream cheese moistened with sufficient cream to handle. Place three or four of these in the inside of the lettuce. Dust with paprika and serve with any desired dressing.

THE CARDINAL'S SALAD

Wash a good lettuce and a bunch of water-cress. Cut a cold boiled beef into strips, add six radishes, two hard-boiled eggs chopped up, and one small sliced cucumber. Arrange the lettuce-leaves in a salad-bowl, mix the other ingredients with a sufficient quantity of mayonnaise sauce, put them in the midst of the lettuce, and serve.

FISH SALADS

FISH SALAD -1

- Cold Boiled Fish
- 1 Lettuce
- 1 Egg
- Salad Dressing

flake up the fish free from skin and bone. Wash and dry the lettuce and shred it up, mix the fish with salad dressing. Put a layer of lettuce at the bottom of the bowl, then one of fish and dressing. Do this alternatively, leaving plenty of lettuce for the top; garnish with hard boiled eggs cut into slices.

FISH SALAD -2
(Salmon or Tuna fish)

- 1 can salmon or tunny (or tuna) fish
- 1 cupful shredded cabbage or sliced celery

Drain the oil from the fish; remove the bone and bits of skin. Add the cabbage or celery, and Mayonnaise or Cream Salad Dressing. Arrange on lettuce and garnish as desired. If Cream Dressing is used with salmon, the oil drained from the salmon may be used for the fat of Cream

Dressing. The salmon may be marinated before adding the other ingredients. When this is done, the salad dressing may be omitted. Salmon contains so much fat that it is not well to add more oil after marinating.

FISH SALAD -3

Cut in small pieces any cold dressed fish, turbot or salmon are the best suited; mix it with half a pint of small salad, and a lettuce cut small, two onions boiled till tender and mild, and a few truffles thinly sliced; pour over a fine salad mixture, and arrange it into a shape, high in the centre, and garnish with hard eggs cut in slices; a little cucumber mixed with the salad is an improvement. The mixture may either be a common salad mixture, or made as follows: take the yolks of three hard boiled eggs, with a spoonful of mustard, and a little salt, mix these with a cup of cream, and four table-spoonsful of vinegar, the different ingredients should be added carefully and worked together smoothly, the whites of the eggs may be trimmed and placed in small heaps round the dish as a garnish.

TUNA FISH SALAD.

A salad that is both attractive and appetizing can be made by using tuna fish as a foundation. This fish, which is grayish-white in color, can be obtained in cans like salmon. As it is not high in price, it gives the housewife another opportunity to provide her family with an inexpensive p r o t e i n d i s h .

- 1 c. tuna fish
- 1/2 c. diced celery
- 1 c. diced cucumber
- Salt and pepper
- Vinegar Lettuce
- Mayonnaise

Open a can of tuna fish, measure 1 cupful, and place in a bowl. Dice the celery and cucumber, mix with the fish, and sprinkle with salt and pepper. Dilute some vinegar with water, using half as much water as vinegar, and sprinkle enough of this over the mixture to flavor it slightly. Allow the mixture to stand for about 1/2 hour in a refrigerator or some other cold place and just before serving pour off this liquid. Heap the salad on lettuce leaves, pour a spoonful of mayonnaise over each portion, and serve.

SALMON SALAD.

Persons who are fond of salmon will find salmon salad a very agreeable dish. In addition to affording a means of varying the diet, this salad makes a comparatively cheap high-protein dish that is suitable for either supper or luncheon.

- 2 c. salmon
- 1 c. diced celery
- 1/4 c. diced Spanish onion
- 3 or 4 sweet pickles, chopped fine
- French dressing
- Salad dressing
- Lettuce

Look the salmon over carefully, removing any skin and bones. Break into medium-sized pieces and mix carefully with the celery, onion, and chopped pickles. Marinate this with the French dressing, taking care not to break up the salmon. Drain and serve with any desired salad dressing on salad plates garnished with lettuce.

MACKEREL SALAD.

Pour boiling water over a large mackerel and let stand for ten minutes; take out and dry thoroughly by draining on a sieve or clean towel. Remove the head, tail and fins, and skin and bones. Shred the fish finely and mix with one large onion, well chopped. Add mustard, vinegar, and pepper to taste. Serve as salad, with young lettuce leaves, and garnish with hard-boiled eggs, sliced. This is a delightful relish with thin-sliced bread and butter.

SARDINE SALAD

- 1/2 tin Sardines
- 2 Eggs
- 1 Lettuce
- Salad Dressings

Split the sardines open and remove the bone. Break some of the lettuce into a bowl, lay on this the sardines. Chop up one of the eggs and sprinkle over them, pour on the dressing. Cover with the rest of the lettuce, and garnish with the other egg cut in slices, and a little watercress or beet root.

CRAB SALAD -1

Boil three dozen hard-shell crabs twenty-five minutes; drain and let them cool gradually; remove the upper shell and the tail, break the remainder apart and pick out the meat carefully. The large claws should not be forgotten, for they contain a dainty morsel, and the creamy fat attached to the upper shell should not be overlooked. Line a salad bowl with the small white leaves of two heads of lettuce, add the crab meat, pour over it a "Mayonnaise" garnish with crab claws, hard-boiled eggs and little mounds of cress leaves, which may be mixed with the salad when served.

CRAB SALAD -2

Crab meat may be either fresh or canned, but, of course, fresh crab meat is more desirable if it can be obtained.

- 2 c. crab meat
- 1 c. diced celery French dressing
- Lettuce
- Mayonnaise
- 1 hard-cooked egg

Chill crab meat and add the diced celery. Marinate with French dressing, and allow this mixture to stand for 1/2 hour or so before serving. Keep as cold as possible. Drain off the French dressing and heap the salad mixture on garnished salad plates or in a salad bowl garnished with lettuce. Pour mayonnaise dressing over the top, garnish with slices of hard-cooked egg, and serve.

SHRIMP SALAD.

Shrimps may be used in an attractive salad in the manner. Persons who care for sea food find this a most appetizing dish. Like lobster and crab, shrimp may be purchased in cans, and so it is possible to have this salad at any season.

First marinate the shrimps with French dressing and then heap them on a plate garnished with lettuce leaves. Add thin slices of hard-cooked egg whites, and place a tender heart of celery in the center of the plate. If desired, some thin slices of celery may be marinated with the shrimp. Serve with mayonnaise dressing.

Salads and Salad Dressing Recipes

PRAWN SALAD

- 1 pint Prawns
- 6 Tomatoes
- Mayonnaise or Salad Dressing
- Pick the prawns, leaving the skin on a few fine ones for a garnish. Peel and slice up the tomatoes and arrange them on a dish; put over them the prawns, and pour over all some mayonnaise or salad dressing. Place the other prawns round as a garnish with a few lettuce leaves broken up.

LOBSTER SALAD -1

Lobster meat may be either fresh or canned, but, of course, fresh lobster meat is more desirable if it can be obtained.

- 2 c. lobster meat
- 1 c. diced celery French dressing
- Lettuce
- Mayonnaise
- 1 hard-cooked egg

Chill lobster meat and add the diced celery. Marinate with French dressing, and allow this mixture to stand for 1/2 hour or so before serving. Keep as cold as possible. Drain off the French dressing and heap the salad mixture on garnished salad plates or in a salad bowl garnished with lettuce. Pour mayonnaise dressing over the top, garnish with slices of hard- cooked egg, and serve. Sufficient to Serve Six.

LOBSTER SALAD -2

Lobsters are done when they assume a red color, which will only require a few minutes hard boiling. Remove the skin and bones, pick to pieces with a fork, marinate them, i.e., place in a dish and season with salt, pepper and a little oil, plenty of vinegar and a little onion cut up; then cover and let stand two or three hours. Cut up hard boiled eggs for a border, line the bottom of the dish with lettuce leaves, place the lobster on the dish in a ring. Mayonnaise can be used if desired, but the lobster is excellent without it.

OYSTER SALAD

- 1 bottle Oysters
- 1 Lettuce
- Half a Lemon
- Mayonnaise or Salad Dressing

Strain away the liquor from a bottle of oysters; put it into a saucepan, and when it boils put in the oysters and cook for five minutes; let them get cold in the liquor. Wash and break up the lettuce and put some of the bottom of a bowl. Strain the liquor from the oysters and mix a little with the dressing, stir in the oysters and spread over the lettuce. Cover with more lettuce and garnish with slices of lemon and red radishes.

MEAT SALADS

CHICKEN SALAD -1

A favored means of using left-over chicken is to make chicken salad of it. It is well, however, if the chicken can be prepared especially for the salad and the nicer pieces of meat used. This is usually done when chicken salad is to be served at a party or special dinner.

- 2 c. chicken
- 1 c. diced celery 1 green pepper French dressing
- Lettuce
- Mayonnaise
- 1 pimiento

Cut the meat from the bones of a chicken and dice it. Dice the celery, clean the green pepper, and cut it into small pieces. Mix the pepper and the celery with the chicken. Marinate with French dressing, chill, and allow to stand for about 1/2 hour. Drain the dressing from the salad mixture, serve in a garnished salad bowl or on garnished salad plates, pour mayonnaise over the top, and garnish with strips of pimiento.

CHICKEN SALAD -2

Take one fowl (boiled); one cucumber; two heads lettuce; two beets (boiled).

Dressing made according to the following recipe:
One teaspoonful mixed mustard; one-half teaspoonful sugar; four tablespoonfuls salad oil; four tablespoonfuls milk; two tablespoonfuls vinegar; cayenne and salt to taste; add the oil, drop by drop, to the mustard and sugar, mixing carefully; next add milk and vinegar gradually, lest the sauce curdle, and the seasoning. Place the shredded chicken on a bed of lettuce, and pour the dressing over it. Around the edge arrange rings of hard boiled eggs, sliced cucumber a n d beet root.

CHICKEN SALAD -3

INGREDIENTS: The remains of cold roast or boiled chicken, 2 lettuces, a little endive, 1 cucumber, a few slices of boiled beetroot and salad-dressing. trim neatly the remains of the chicken; wash, dry, and slicethe lettuces, and place in the middle of a dish; put the pieces of fowl on the top, and pour the salad-dressing over them. Garnish the edge of the salad with hard-boiled eggs cut in rings, sliced cucumber, and boiled beetroot cut in slices. Instead of cutting the eggs in rings, the yolks may be rubbed through a hair sieve, and the whites chopped very finely, and arranged on the salad in small bunches, yellow and white alternately. This should not be made long before it is wanted for table.

CHICKEN SALAD -4

As the Irishman would say, turkey makes the best chicken salad. Boil till well done. Use only the white meat, which cut with sharp scissors into pieces about one-half inch square; add an equal quantity of celery cut in same manner, sprinkling over it salt and pepper. Put in a cold place till two hours before serving, then add the following dressing:
For one chicken take three eggs, one cup of vinegar, one cup of sweet milk, one-half cup butter, one tablespoon made mustard, salt, black and red pepper, beat eggs, melt butter; stir all together over a slow fire till it thickens; when cool beat into it one cup of cream.
Serve salad on crisp, well-bleached lettuce leaves, on the top of each putting a small quantity of mayonnaise dressing.

SOUTHERN CHICKEN SALAD.

Cut one chicken into small pieces (not too small); boil one egg hard and pulverize the yolk (cut the white into the chicken); add the beaten yolks of three raw eggs; one-half teaspoonful each of ground mustard, white pepper, salt, sugar and celery salt or seed, the juice of one lemon, one tablespoonful melted butter, one tablespoonful salad oil (some prefer all butter); beat all well together until light and pour into one gill of boiling vinegar and let all cook until thick as cream, stirring constantly to avoid curdling. When cold, pour over your chicken, to which has been added as much chopped celery, and salt and pepper to taste.

CHICKEN SALAD (HAWAIIAN)

This recipe is good for a summer lunch. You should keep it cold until serving, but contrary to popular belief, mayonnaise itself isn't particularly dangerous from a food safety point of view. Mayonnaise in its usual commercial formulations is acid enough to be mildly protective against harmful microorganisms. But it's not protective enough, so don't take chances and do keep this refrigerated until you need it. 6 cups cooked chicken, cut in chunks

- 1-1/2 cups mayonnaise or salad dressing
- 2 cups chopped celery
- 2 tablespoons soy sauce
- 1 can pineapple tidbits, drained
- 1/2 cup slivered almonds, lightly toasted, divided In a large mixing bowl combine chicken, mayonnaise, celery and soy sauce. Gently fold in pineapple and half of almond slivers. Serve salad on a platter lined with lettuce leaves. Garnish with remaining almonds. Serves 12 to 15.

CHICKEN SPRING SALAD

Spinach is an excellent source of Vitamins A and C, as well as potassium and magnesium. When you eat it uncooked, as in this recipe, dentists say spinach is a detergent food, helpful to d e n t a l h ea l t h .

- 3 cups cooked chicken, cut in chunks
- 1 package (10-ounces) raw spinach, washed and drained with stems removed and torn into
- small pieces
- 1 small clove garlic, minced
- 1 tablespoon chives, snipped, fresh or frozen

Salads and Salad Dressing Recipes

- 1 tea spoon salt or to taste
- 1/8 teaspoon ground pepper
- 1 teaspoon sugar
- 3/4 cup chopped pecans
- 2 apples, chopped
- 1/2 cup oil
- 1/4 cup red wine vinegar
- In a salad bowl combine all ingredients and toss lightly. Serves 6 to 8.

FRENCH DRESSING CHICKEN SALAD

This is a real "fast food," perfect for when you've got a lot of other things to do besides fuss in the kitchen. It's quick and easy, but the Cayenne pepper gives it a little perk that lifts it out of the ordinary.

- 2 cups cooked, diced chicken
- 1/2 cup finely chopped celery
- 1/4 cup French dressing
- 1/4 cup mayonnaise or salad dressing
- 1/8 teaspoon Cayenne pepper

In a salad bowl toss together all ingredients and serve on lettuce. Serves 3-4

OLIVEY CHICKEN SALAD

- 2 cups cooked, diced chicken
- 1 cup cooked rice (1/4 cup uncooked yields 1 cup cooked)
- 3/4 cup chopped celery
- 1/2 cup sliced pimento-stuffed green olives
- 1/4 cup toasted slivered almonds
- 1/4 cup thinly sliced scallions
- 1 tea spoon salt or to taste
- 1/4 teaspoon ground pepper
- 1/2 cup mayonnaise or salad dressing
- 2 tablespoons fresh lemon juice

In a mixing bowl combine all ingredients and serve salad on a bed of lettuce leaves. Serves 4 to 6.

SUNSHINE CHICKEN SALAD

The avocado you use in this recipe should be fully ripe, and that means it will have a slight give to it when you press it between your palms. If it has about as much "give" to it as a baseball, let it ripen for a couple of days more at room temperature. But don't refrigerate it because refrigeration puts a permanent stop to all ripening.

- 3 cups cooked, diced chicken
- 1 can (6-ounces) orange juice concentrate
- 3 table spoon soil
- 1 tablespoon vinegar
- 1 tablespoon sugar
- 1/4 teaspoon dry mustard
- 1/4 teaspoon salt or to taste
- 1/8 teaspoon Tabasco 1 cup chopped celery
- 1/2 cup diced ripe olives
- 1 medium avocado, cut in small chunks
- 1/4 cup toasted, slivered almonds

In a blender or food processor, make dressing by blending orange juice concentrate, oil, vinegar, sugar, dry mustard, salt and Tabasco at high speed 5 seconds or until smooth. In a salad bowl combine chicken, celery, olives, avocado and almonds. Pour dressing over. Toss and chill at least 30 minutes before serving. Serves 4 to 5.

CORNED BEEF SALAD

- Slices of Corned Beef
- 1 Lettuce
- 2 Eggs
- Mayonnaise or Salad Dressing

Take some slices of cold corned beef, dip them in a salad dressing, and lay them in a dish with alternate layers of lettuce leaves. Garnish with hard boiled eggs cut in slices.

MUTTON CARROT SALAD

- 2 o r 3 Cold Boiled Carrots
- 1/2 lb. Cold Boiled Mutton
- 1 stalk Celery
- 6 Capers
- Half a teaspoonful Parsley
- Salad Dressing

Cut up some cold boiled mutton into small pieces and lay them in a salad bowl. Mince up the celery and capers and strew over it, then pour over the dressing. Slice up the cold carrots and lay them on top; garnish with the chopped parsley, and serve.

SOUP MEAT SALAD

The meat which has been boiled down for soup makes a nice salad. When the stock has been poured off, press the meat into a basin with about a gill of jelly stock, and some salt and pepper. When cold and firm, cut it into neat pieces and lay in a salad bowl. Pour over it some remoulade sauce and shred on top some nice white lettuce leaves; it may be garnished with beetroot or hard boiled eggs.

LAMB SALAD

- Cold Roast Lamb
- 2 Lettuces 1 T o ma t o 12 Capers
- 2 Eggs
- Remoulade Dressing

Cut the lamb into small pieces and lay it in a bowl. Cut the tomato into thin slices and lay it over, then the capers chopped small. Pour over the dressing, break up the lettuces and put over, and garnish with the hard boiled eggs cut in slices.

ITALIAN MEAT SALAD -1

- 1 Salt Herring
- Cold slices of Meat
- 1 teaspoonful Mustard
- 1 B e e t r o o t
- 4 tablespoonsful Oil
- 3 tablespoonsful Tarragon Vinegar
- 1/2 oz. Capers
- 3 Boiled Potatoes

Wash the herring in cold water and soak it in milk for an hour; cut it open and take out the bone and slice up both the fish and the meat. Arrange in a bowl, chop the capers and put over. Put the mustard into a basin, add gradually the oil and vinegar; pour this, when well mixed, over the fish and meat, and cover with slices of cold potatoes. Garnish with any cold vegetables in the larder or with some green pickles from a bottle of pickles, a little chopped parsley, and some small radishes.

ITALIAN MEAT SALAD -2

Cut up the white parts of a cold fowl, and mix it with mustard and cress, and a lettuce chopped finely, and pour over a fine salad mixture, composed of equal quantities of vinegar and the finest salad oil, salt, mustard, and the yolks of hard boiled eggs, and the yolk of one raw egg, mixed smoothly together; a little tarragon vinegar is then added, and the mixture is poured over the salad; the whites of the eggs are mixed, and serve to garnish the dish, arranged in small heaps alternately with heaps of grated smoked beef; two or three hard boiled eggs are cut up with the chicken in small pieces and mixed with the salad. The appearance of this salad may be varied by piling the fowl in the centre of the dish, then pour over the salad mixture, and make a wall of any dressed salad, laying the whites of the eggs (after the yolks have been removed for the mixture), cut in rings on the top like a chain.

GROUSE SALAD.

INGREDIENTS: 8 eggs, butter, fresh salad, 1 or 2 grouse; for the sauce, 1 teaspoonful of minced shalot, 1 teaspoonful of pounded sugar, the yolk of 1 egg, 1 teaspoonful of minced parsley, 1/4 oz. of salt, 4 tablespoonfuls of oil, 2 tablespoonfuls of Chili vinegar, 1 gill of cream.

Boil the eggs hard, shell them, throw them into cold water cut a thin slice off the bottom to facilitate the proper placing of them in the dish, cut each one into four lengthwise, and make a very thin flat border of butter, about one inch from the edge of the dish the salad is to be served on; fix the pieces of egg upright close to each other, the yolk outside, or the yolk and white alternately; lay in the centre a fresh salad of whatever is in season, and, having previously roasted the grouse rather underdone, cut it into eight or ten pieces, and prepare the sauce as follows:

Put the shalots into a basin, with the sugar, the yolk of an egg, the parsley, and salt, and mix in by degrees the oil and vinegar; when these ingredients are well mixed, put the sauce on ice or in a cool place. When ready to serve, whip the cream rather thick, which lightly mix with it; then lay the inferior parts of the grouse on the salad, sauce over so as to cover each piece, then lay over the salad and the remainder of the grouse, pour the rest of the sauce over, and serve. The eggs may be ornamented with a little dot of radishes or beetroot on the point. Anchovy and gherkin, cut into small diamonds, may be placed between, or cut gherkins in slices, and a border of them lai round.

OTHER SALADS

BREAD SALAD

- 5 slices Stale Bread
- 1/2 gill Oil
- 3 Pickled Onions
- 1 piece Pickled Cauliflower
- 2 Eggs
- 1 B e e t r o o t
- 2 slices Cold Mutton
- 1 tablespoonful Vinegar
- Mustard and Cress

Trim off the crust and cut the bread into dice, put into a bowl and pour over the oil. Let it stand till all the oil is absorbed; then mince up the onion, cauliflower, eggs, and meat, and strew them over. Season with pepper and salt. Well wash the mustard and cress and arrange on the top. Cut the beetroot into neat shapes and arrange as a garnish.

CHESTNUT SALAD

Equal parts of boiled chestnuts and shredded celery are combined. Bananas, apples, celery and chestnuts. Dress with mayonnaise and serve on lettuce leaves.

SWEETBREAD SALAD

Take cucumbers and cut lengthwise to serve the salad in; scrape out the inside and salt well, then squeeze and use this to mix with the filling. Take a pair of sweetbreads, or calf's brains, wash well, and boil; when done, throw in cold water at once and skim them; chop fine, add bunch of celery, one can of French peas, scraped part of cucumber; mix all together and season. Make a mayonnaise, mix with it, and fill the cucumber shells; keep all cold, and serve on lettuce leaf.

NEAPOLITAN SALAD

Take some white meat of a turkey, cut up fine, cut up a few pickles the same way, a few beets, one or two carrots, a few potatoes (the carrots and potatoes must be parboiled), also a few stalks of asparagus; chop up a bunch of crisp, white celery; a whole celery root (parboiled), sprinkle all with fine salt and pour a mayonnaise dressing over it. Line the salad bowl with lettuce leaves or white cabbage leaves. Add a few hard-boiled eggs and capers; garnish with sprigs of fresh parsley.

SPANISH SALAD.

Put into the centre of the bowl some cold dressed French beans or scarlet runners, and before serving pour over some good mayonnaise. Garnish the beans with three tomatoes cut in slices and arranged in a circle one overlapping the other.

VARIOUS SALAD DRESSINGS AND THEIR PREPARATIONS

Various salad dressings may be made to serve with salads. The kind of dressing to select depends both on the variety of salad served and on the personal preference of those to whom it is served. Some of these contain only a few ingredients and are comparatively simple to make, while others are complex and involve considerable work in their making. Whether simple or elaborate, however, the salad dressing

Salads and Salad Dressing Recipes

should be carefully chosen, so that it will blend well with the ingredients of the salad with which it is used.

A number of recipes for salad dressings are here given. They are taken up before the recipes for salads so that the beginner will be familiar with the different varieties when they are mentioned in connection with the salads. As many of the recipes as possible should be tried, not only for the knowledge that will be gained, but also for the practical experience.

FRENCH DRESSING -1

Mix 1 tablespoon lemon juice or vinegar, 1/2 teaspoon salt, 1/8
teaspoon pepper or few grains cayenne pepper in bowl; add 3 to 4 tablespoons olive oil, beating constantly. Place on ice until ready to serve.

FRENCH DRESSING -2

A dressing that is very simply made and that can probably be used with a greater variety of salads than any other is French dressing. For instance, it may be used with any vegetable salad, with salads containing almost any combination of fruit, and with meat, fish, and egg salads.

- 3/4 tsp. salt
- 1/4 tsp. mustard 1/4 tsp. pepper
- 3 Tb. vinegar
- 1/4 tsp. paprika
- 1/2 c. oil

Measure the dry ingredients and place them in a bowl. Measure the vinegar and oil and add them to the dry ingredients. If possible, place a piece of ice the size of a walnut in the bowl. Beat with a fork until the ingredients are thoroughly mixed and the oil and vinegar form an emulsion that will remain for a short time. The ingredients will separate if the dressing is allowed to stand, but the colder they are, the more easily will the emulsion form and the longer will it remain. If ice cannot be used, have the ingredients as cold as possible before mixing them.

CREAM SALAD DRESSING -1

A simple dressing that requires very little time or skill in preparation and that affords a means of using up cream that has soured is the one given in the accompanying recipe. Sweet cream may also be used in the same way if desired, and this makes an excellent dressing for cabbage salad, plain cucumber salad with lettuce, or fruit salad. If the dressing is to be used for fruit salad, lemon juice may be used in the place of vinegar.

- 1 c. sour cream
- 1/2 tsp. salt 2 Tb. sugar
- 1/4 c. vinegar

Whip the cream with a rotary beater until it is stiff. Then add the sugar, salt, and vinegar, and continue beating until the mixture is well blended. Cool and serve.

Cream Salad Dressing -2

Two eggs, three table-spoonfuls of vinegar, one of cream, one teaspoonful of sugar, one-fourth of a teaspoonful of salt, one-fourth of a teaspoonful of mustard. Beat two eggs well. Add the sugar, salt and mustard, then the vinegar, and the cream. Place the bowl in a basin of boiling water, and stir until about the thickness of rich cream. If the bowl is thick and the water boils all the time, it will take about five minutes. Cool, and use as needed.

SOUR CREAM DRESSING -1

Sour-cream dressing is not a very economical one to make unless there happens to be sour cream on hand. It is, however, a very good dressing for both fruit and vegetable salad.

- 2 T b . butter
- 1/3 c. vinegar
- 3 Tb. flour
- 1 c. sour cream
- 2 Tb. sugar
- 2 eggs
- 1 tsp. salt
- 1 c. whipped cream

Salads and Salad Dressing Recipes

Melt the butter in the upper part of a double boiler, add the flour, sugar, salt, vinegar, and sour cream. Cook together over the flame until the mixture thickens. Beat the egg yolks and add them to this. Place in the lower part of the double boiler and cook until the egg yolks thicken. Beat the egg whites and fold them with the whipped cream into the salad dressing. Cool and serve.

SOUR CREAM DRESSING -2

Mix one cup of sour cream and three eggs, well beaten. Dissolve two tablespoons of sugar and one tablespoon of mustard in one-half cup of vinegar; salt, pepper and paprika to taste, and then stir this slowly into the cream and eggs. Put in double boiler, cook until thick, then add butter the size of an egg and cook about five minutes longer. Take from fire and bottle; this dressing will keep for months.

MAYONNAISE DRESSING -1

Although mayonnaise dressing is prepared without the application of heat, it is not one of the simplest dressings to prepare. It meets with much favor, being used almost as extensively as French dressing, but it is perhaps less desirable with fruit salads than with others. It is also much used as a basis for numerous other dressings. Before serving, it may be thinned by beating either sweet or sour cream into it. It may be made fluffy and light and its quantity may be increased by beating whipped cream into it.

- 1/2 tsp. salt
- 2 egg yolks
- 1/4 tsp. pepper
- 1-1/2 c. oil
- 1/4 tsp. mustard
- 4 Tb. vinegar or lemon juice

Mix the dry ingredients in a bowl. Separate the eggs and add the yolks to the dry ingredients. Beat these with a rotary egg beater until they are well mixed. To this mixture, add a few drops of oil and continue to beat. Add a drop of the vinegar or lemon juice, a few more drops of oil, and beat constantly. Gradually increase the quantity of oil added each time, but do not do this rapidly. As the oil is added and the beating is continued, it will be noted that the mixture grows thicker, but when vinegar is added the mixture is thinned. The quantity of vinegar is so much less than that of oil that the oil may be added in small amounts two or three times in succession before vinegar is added.

This process is rather long and slow, but if the mixing is done correctly, the result will be a thick, smooth mixture that will not separate for possibly 6 or 7 days. Mayonnaise mixers, which may be procured for making this dressing, make the work easier, but they are not at all necessary. Mayonnaise may be made as successfully with a bowl and a rotary beater, if it will just be remembered that the liquid ingredients must be added slowly and that they must be as cold a s possible.

MAYONNAISE DRESSING -2

- 1 egg yolk
- 1/2 teaspoon dry mustard
- 1/2 teaspoon salt
- 1/16 teaspoon cayenne pepper
- 1 cup salad oil
- 2 tablespoons vinegar or lemon juice

Utensils and ingredients should be very cold. Put egg yolk into shallow bowl; add, seasoning and mix well; add oil slowly, almost drop by drop, beating continually until very thick. Thin with vinegar; continue adding oil and vinegar until all is used.

MAYONNAISE DRESSING -3

- 1 egg
- juice of 1 lemon or 4 tablespoons vinegar
- 1 tea spoon salt
- 1/4 teaspoon paprika
- few grains cayenne
- 2 cups salad oil

Put egg with vinegar or lemon juice and seasoning into bowl and beat with rotary egg beater. Add oil a tablespoonful or more at a time, beating constantly. Well covered, this mayonnaise will keep for three or four weeks.

COOKED MAYONNAISE.

A dressing that is very similar both in texture and taste to the mayonnaise just explained and perhaps a little easier to make is known as cooked mayonnaise. This dressing, as will be noted from the accompanying recipe, may be made in larger quantities than the Uncooked mayonnaise.

- 2 Tb. oil
- 1/4 tsp. mustard
- 4 Tb. flour
- 1/4 tsp. paprika
- 1/2 c. vinegar
- 2 eggs
- 1 c. boiling water
- 2 c. oil
- 1 T b. salt

Mix the 2 tablespoonfuls of oil and the flour and pour in the vinegar. Add the boiling water and stir the mixture until it is perfectly smooth and well mixed. Place over the fire and cook for about 5 minutes. Remove from the fire and cool. When completely cooled, add the salt, mustard, and paprika. Separate the eggs and beat the yolks and whites separately. Add the egg yolks to the mixture. Add the 2 cupfuls of oil a little at a time, beating thoroughly with a rotary beater each time oil is added. When all of this is completely mixed and thoroughly beaten, fold in the stiffly beaten egg whites.

MAYONNAISE WITH WHIPPED CREAM

When you are in want of a large quantity of dressing, mayonnaise or French, add one pint of whipped cream to your prepared dressing, stirring thoroughly, just before ready to serve.

WHITE MAYONNAISE

To make white mayonnaise, follow the ordinary directions, using lemon juice instead of vinegar, omitting the mustard and adding, when finished, a half cup of whipped cream or half an egg white beaten very stiff.

Red Mayonnaise Dressing.

Lobster "coral" is pounded to a powder, rubbed through a sieve, and mixed with mayonnaise dressing. This gives a dressing of a bright color. Or, the juice from boiled beets can be used instead of "coral."

Green Mayonnaise Dressing.

Mix enough spinach green with mayonnaise sauce to give it a bright green color. A little finely-chopped parsley can be added.

RUSSIAN SALAD DRESSING

Make one-half pint of mayonnaise dressing and add to it the following: Two hard-boiled eggs chopped fine, two to four tablespoons of tomato catsup, one tablespoon of finely chopped parsley, one teaspoon of finely chopped or grated white onion or shallot, after these ingredients are mixed, fold them into one cup of mayonnaise and serve. Enough for ten people.

BOILED SALAD DRESSING -1

- 1/2 tablespoon salt
- 1-1/2 tablespoons sugar
- 1 tea spoon mustard 1/2 tablespoon flour
- few grains cayenne
- 1/2 cup vinegar
- 2 eggs
- 3/4 cup milk
- 1 table spoon butter or other shortening

Mix dry ingredients in top of double boiler; add vinegar and beaten egg yolks and mix; add milk and butter. Cook in double boiler until thick and smooth. Take from fire and add beaten egg whites. Cool and serve.

BOILED SALAD DRESSING -2

Although boiled salad dressing is not so great a favorite as the uncooked mayonnaise dressing, it has the advantage of being less expensive. Then, too, it is one of the dressings that may be made without oil, and so finds favor with those to whom oil is not agreeable. However, oil may be substituted for the butter that is given in the recipe. It will be noted that the preparation of this dressing is similar to that of a custard with the addition of flour. Since the flour requires longer cooking than the eggs, they are added last so that there will be no danger of overcooking them. If the dressing curdles, it may be known that the eggs have cooked too long, but this condition may be remedied by placing the pan containing the dressing in a pan of cold water as soon as the curdling is observed and then beating vigorously with a rotary beater.

- 2 Tb. butter
- 1 tsp. mustard
- 2 Tb. flour
- 1 c. milk
- 1 t sp . salt
- 2 eggs
- 2 tsp. sugar
- 1/4 c. vinegar

Melt the butter in the inner pan of a double boiler, add the flour, salt, sugar, mustard, and milk. Cook over the flame until the mixture is thickened. Beat the eggs, stir them into the mixture, and add the vinegar, beating rapidly. Place in the large pan of the double boiler and allow this to cook until the eggs have thickened. Cool and serve.

THOUSAND ISLAND DRESSING.

By using the cooked or the uncooked mayonnaise dressing as a basis and adding to it the ingredients listed here, a very delightful salad dressing, called Thousand Island dressing, is the result. All the ingredients need not be added if it is inconvenient to do so, still the dressing is better when they are all used. This dressing is particularly good when served with plain lettuce salad, with lettuce and tomatoes, with lettuce, tomatoes, and cucumbers, or with any other plain-vegetable salad.

- 1 c. mayonnaise dressing
- 2 Tb. chopped green pepper
- 1/4 c. chilli sauce
- 1 Tb. chopped onion
- 2 Tb. chopped pimento
- 1 hard-cooked egg

Into the mayonnaise stir the chilli sauce, pimiento, pepper, and onion, and lastly, add the hard-cooked egg chopped into fine pieces. Chill and serve.

MUSTARD DRESSING

Take yolk of one hard-boiled egg and rub smooth in a bowl. Add two teaspoons of French mustard, salt, pepper, and little sugar. Add a little oil, and then a little vinegar. Garnish top with the white, cut in pieces.

Salad Dressing Without Oil.

The yolks of four uncooked eggs, one table-spoonful of salt, one heaping teaspoonful of sugar, one heaping teaspoonful of mustard, half a cupful of clarified chicken fat, a quarter of a cupful of vinegar, the juice of half a lemon, a speck of cayenne. Make as directed for mayonnaise dressing.

Salad Dressing made with Butter.

Four table-spoonfuls of butter, one of flour, one table-spoonful of salt, one of sugar, one heaping teaspoonful of mustard, a speck of cayenne, one cupful of milk, half a cupful of vinegar, three eggs. Let the butter get hot in a sauce-pan. Add the flour, and stir until smooth, being careful not to brown. Add the milk, and boil up. Place the sauce-pan in another of hot water. Beat the eggs, salt, pepper, sugar and mustard together, and add the vinegar. Stir this into the boiling mixture, and stir until it thickens like soft custard, which will be in about fire minutes. Set away to cool; and when cold, bottle, and place in the ice-chest. This will keep two weeks.

EAST INDIAN SALAD SAUCE

- 2 Eggs.
- 1 teaspoonful Curry Powder
- 1/2 gill Oil
- 1/4 gill Vinegar

Boil the eggs hard; put the yolks into a bowl and work them till they are quite smooth. Work in gradually the curry powder, oil, and vinegar. Blend well, and it is ready. It may be used sometimes instead of mayonnaise or ordinary salad dressing.

Maple Tree Books

If you want to get access to upcoming books on various topics, 'like' our Facebook page to be informed. We always ofer the books for free for 5 days when they are first released.
You can download them when they are free and benefit from them :)
Go to this website and enter your name and email to join our mailing list.
https://www.Facebook.com/mapletreebooks
And oh, dont forget to leave a review :)

Even if you did not benefit from this book at all we s ll want to hear from your feedback so we can improve in the future :)

Alternatively you can join our mailing list

http://www.MapleTreeBooks.com
You can join our Twitter page as well https://Twitter.com/MapleTreeBooks1
Thanks for reading :)

We wish you success in this life and in the next.

Printed in Great Britain
by Amazon